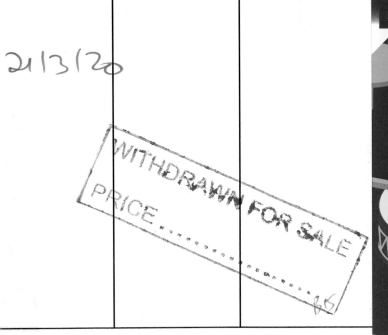

21/3/20

Please renew or return items by the date shown on your receipt

www.hertfordshire.gov.uk/libraries

Renewals and enquiries: 0300 123 4049

Textphone for hearing or 0300 123 4041 speech impaired users:

L32 11.16

Hertfordshire

CONTENTS

WELCOME TO THE WORLD OF INFOGRAPHICS

Using icons, graphics and pictograms, infographics visualise information in a whole new way!

SEE WHICH ANIMALS CAN SURVIVE IN THE DESERTS

FIND OUT HOW COLD THE AIR GETS AS YOU CLIMB A MOUNTAIN

DISCOVER THE DIFFERENT LAYERS OF A RAINFOREST, FROM THE TREE TOPS DOWN TO GROUND LEVEL

WHAT IS A HABITAT?

A habitat is an area where a plant or an animal lives and the conditions found there. The type of habitat depends on a wide range of variables, including the climate, the surrounding features, the position on the planet and the type of rock found there.

56.7°C
HIGHEST RECORDED TEMPERATURE
10 FEBRUARY 1913, FURNACE CREEK, DEATH VALLEY, CALIFORNIA, USA

Types of habitat

Ocean – the largest habitat, covering more than 70 per cent of the planet, it is dominated by salty water and ranges from rich coral reefs to the dark ocean abyss.

Mountains – high altitude habitats that vary the farther up you travel, from lush rainforests to open grassland to bare rock.

Mediterranean – found in regions with hot, dry summers, these regions contain scrub vegetation.

Tropical rainforests – these regions are warm and wet all year round and contain high concentrations and variations of plants and animals.

Temperate grasslands – large areas of grassland found in temperate regions, they support large herds of grazing animals.

Tundra – cold, treeless regions where the ground just below the surface remains frozen all year round. This frozen layer is called permafrost.

Deserts – dry regions of the world that receive very little precipitation throughout the year.

-68°C
LOWEST RECORDED TEMPERATURE
(FOR A PERMANENTLY INHABITED PLACE) 1933, **OYMYAKON, RUSSIA**

Temperate forest – containing a mix of evergreen and deciduous trees, these regions have four distinct seasons every year.

MEGHALAYA IN INDIA RECEIVES

11,873 MM
OF RAIN EVERY YEAR – MORE THAN ANYWHERE ELSE.

IN CONTRAST, SOME SCIENTISTS BELIEVE THAT THE **DRY VALLEYS IN ANTARCTICA** HAVE NOT SEEN RAIN FOR NEARLY

2 MILLION YEARS.

Tropical grassland – areas of large grassland with long dry seasons and short rainy seasons.

Poles – cold regions around the planet's two poles, these areas are covered by thick sheets of ice all year.

TEMPERATE AND EVERGREEN FORESTS

Forests found in cooler regions of the world have short growing periods during the spring and summer months. At other times, plants and animals have to cope with cold, sometimes freezing, temperatures.

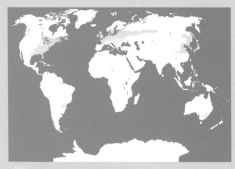

Temperate forest

Temperate forests

These habitats are found in regions of the world lying between the tropics and the polar areas. They have four distinct seasons: spring, summer, autumn and winter. During these seasons, deciduous trees sprout buds which grow into leaves. These then turn brown and fall off during autumn and the tree stands dormant during winter.

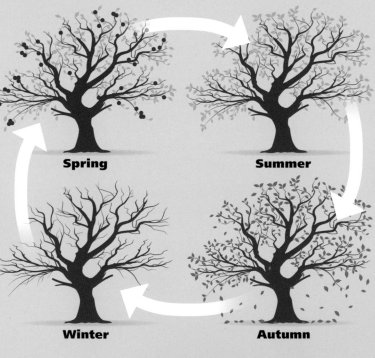

Spring

Summer

Winter

Autumn

Some forests have such a thick canopy (the layer of branches and leaves) that little light reaches the forest floor in summer. This means that few plants grow there.

Plants living in temperate forests include broad-leafed trees, such as oak and beech, as well as ground-flowering plants including bluebells.

Oak

Beech

Bluebells

Hedgehog

Fox

Some animals, such as hedgehogs, hibernate through the cold winter months. Other forest animals include foxes and deer.

Taiga

The northern coniferous forest is also known as the taiga. It is the largest land habitat in the world and covers about 17 per cent of Earth's land surface, mostly in a huge belt that runs across the northern hemisphere.

17%

⬡ **Coniferous forests or taiga**

Plants include conifers and pines, as well as grasses and sedges.

Grasses   **Fir Tree**   **Pine Tree**

Animals living in the taiga have to survive long cold winters and short summers. Some do this by hibernating or entering a long sleep-like state. These include bears. Others travel (migrate) away during the winter and return in the summer. These include geese.

Goose   **Bear**

Temperature and rainfall

Temperate

Average temperatures are about **10°C**, with warm summers averaging about **20°C**.

75–150 cm of rain per year

Taiga

Temperatures range from about **0°C to -10°C** (but can get down to -50°C) in winter and about **15–20°C** in summer.

30–50 cm of rain per year

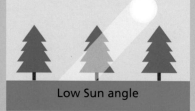

Low Sun angle

The Sun is low in the sky (at an angle of 63.5–47°) because of the northerly latitude so less solar energy reaches the ground. Snow cover also reflects a lot of solar energy.

RAINFORESTS

These are some of the richest habitats on the planet, supporting an enormous range of plants and animals. While most of them are found in warm tropical regions close to the Equator, a handful lie in cooler temperate regions.

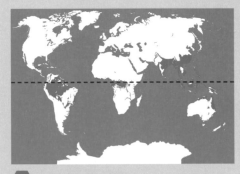

⬡ **Rainforests**

Tropical rainforests

This habitat covers just 6 per cent of Earth, but contains more than half its plant and animal species.

········· Tropical rainforests

6%

MORE THAN 50% Plants and animals

Layers of the rainforest

Emergent – the tallest trees, called emergents, poke above the canopy.

Canopy – the branches and leaves of the trees form a thick layer called the canopy, which lets little light through.

Under canopy – below the canopy, young trees wait for older trees to die so they can take their place, while lianas grow up from the forest floor, using trees for support.

Shrub level and forest floor – very little light reaches the forest floor, restricting the amount of plants that can grow here.

Rainforest plants include exotic flowers, such as pitcher plants and orchids, and huge trees.

Boa constrictor

Orchid

Pitcher plant

Jaguar

Animals include big cats, such as tigers and jaguars, apes, birds of paradise and large snakes, such as boa constrictors.

Temperature and rainfall

Rainforests get more than **250 cm** of rain every year.

= 15 cm

The temperature varies little and stays between **25–30°C** all year round.

TEMPERATE RAINFORESTS

These are found in cooler regions, including North America, East Asia, Australia and New Zealand. They have a long wet season, but also a dry season.

Deer

Plants include tall redwoods, Douglas fir, ferns and mosses. Animals include black bears, deer and cougars.

Douglas fir

92.99 m

Statue of liberty

Redwoods are some of the largest single living things on the planet, and can grow to heights of more than **100 metres.**

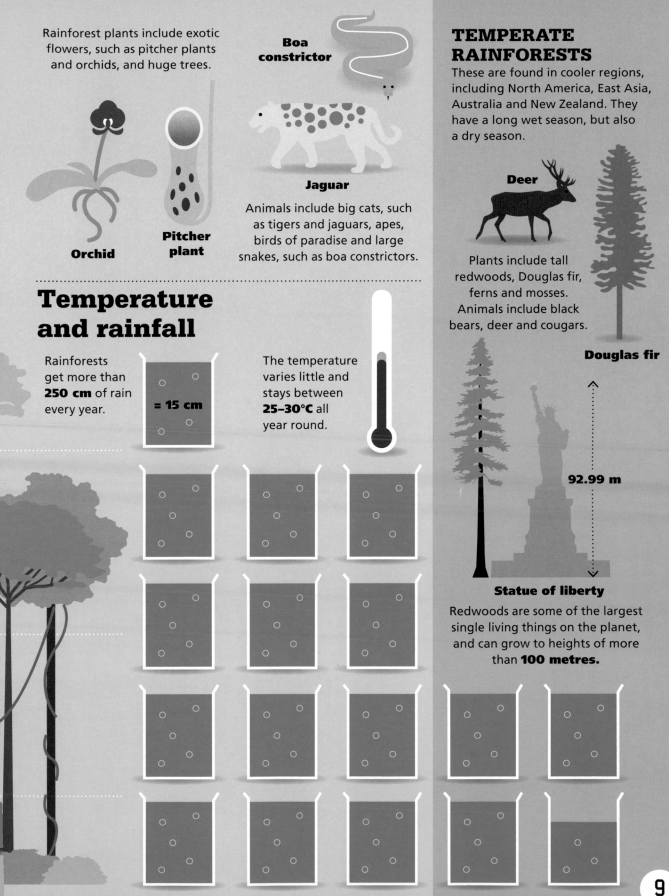

DESERTS

Deserts are regions that receive less than 25 cm of rain in an entire year. Although many of them are found in hot regions close to the Equator, there are also some that lie in cooler temperate regions, where local features and conditions prevent a lot of rainfall.

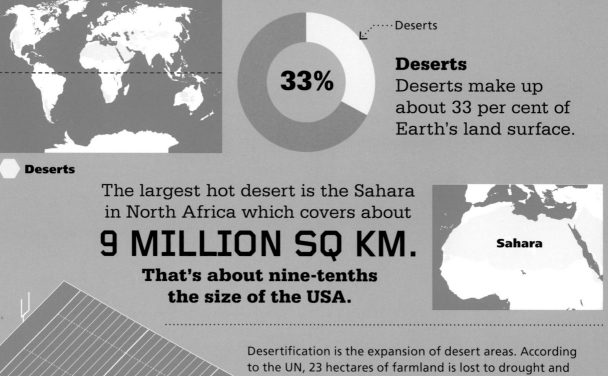

·······Deserts

33%

Deserts
Deserts make up about 33 per cent of Earth's land surface.

⬡ **Deserts**

The largest hot desert is the Sahara in North Africa which covers about

9 MILLION SQ KM.

That's about nine-tenths the size of the USA.

Sahara

Desertification is the expansion of desert areas. According to the UN, 23 hectares of farmland is lost to drought and desertification every single minute! That's the same area as

45 American football fields.

Temperature and rainfall

Hot deserts have an average annual temperature of **20–25°C**, but can get higher than **50°C**. Temperatures at night can fall below **0°C**.

= 15 cm

Deserts get less than **25 cm** of rain every year.

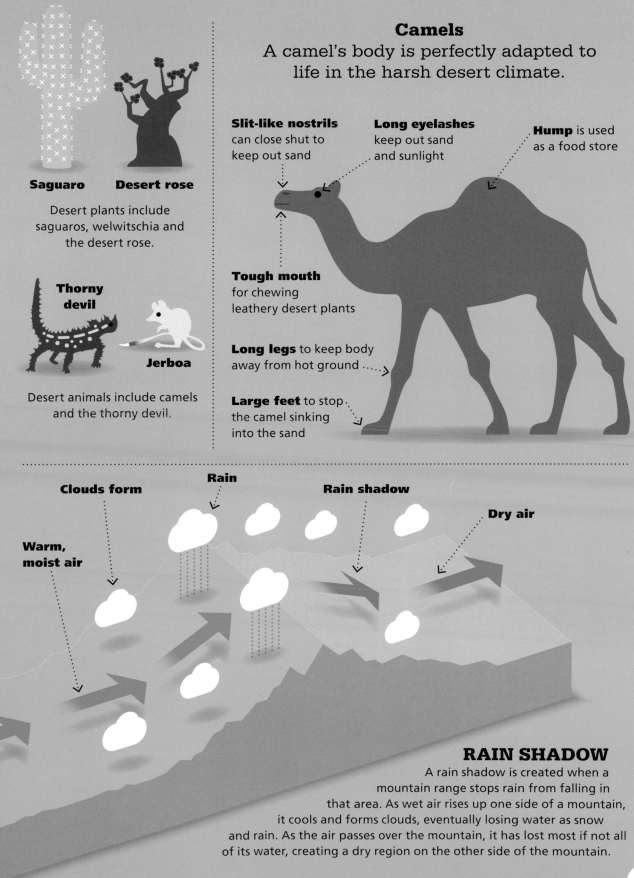

Saguaro   **Desert rose**

Desert plants include saguaros, welwitschia and the desert rose.

Thorny devil

Jerboa

Desert animals include camels and the thorny devil.

Camels
A camel's body is perfectly adapted to life in the harsh desert climate.

Slit-like nostrils can close shut to keep out sand

Long eyelashes keep out sand and sunlight

Hump is used as a food store

Tough mouth for chewing leathery desert plants

Long legs to keep body away from hot ground

Large feet to stop the camel sinking into the sand

Clouds form

Rain

Rain shadow

Dry air

Warm, moist air

RAIN SHADOW
A rain shadow is created when a mountain range stops rain from falling in that area. As wet air rises up one side of a mountain, it cools and forms clouds, eventually losing water as snow and rain. As the air passes over the mountain, it has lost most if not all of its water, creating a dry region on the other side of the mountain.

MOUNTAINS

Because they cover a wide range of altitudes, mountains support a variety of habitats. These vary as the conditions change the higher up the mountain you travel.

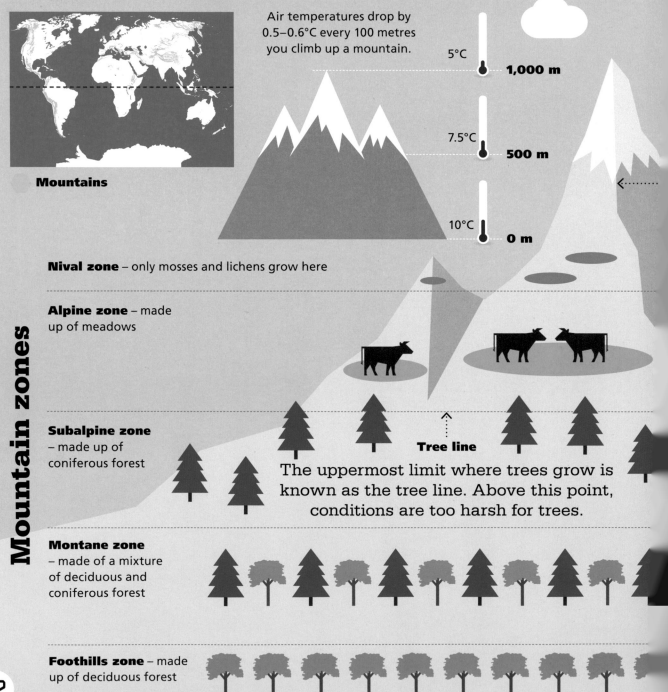

Mountains

Air temperatures drop by 0.5–0.6°C every 100 metres you climb up a mountain.

5°C — **1,000 m**

7.5°C — **500 m**

10°C — **0 m**

Mountain zones

Nival zone – only mosses and lichens grow here

Alpine zone – made up of meadows

Subalpine zone – made up of coniferous forest

Tree line

The uppermost limit where trees grow is known as the tree line. Above this point, conditions are too harsh for trees.

Montane zone – made of a mixture of deciduous and coniferous forest

Foothills zone – made up of deciduous forest

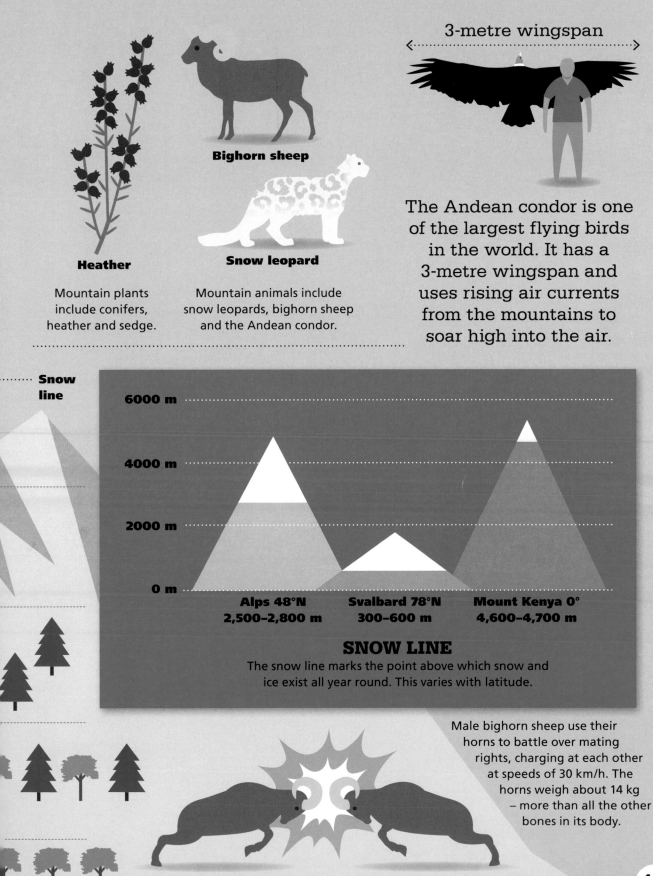

Bighorn sheep

Snow leopard

Heather

3-metre wingspan

The Andean condor is one of the largest flying birds in the world. It has a 3-metre wingspan and uses rising air currents from the mountains to soar high into the air.

Mountain plants include conifers, heather and sedge.

Mountain animals include snow leopards, bighorn sheep and the Andean condor.

Snow line

| 6000 m | 4000 m | 2000 m | 0 m |

Alps 48°N
2,500–2,800 m

Svalbard 78°N
300–600 m

Mount Kenya 0°
4,600–4,700 m

SNOW LINE
The snow line marks the point above which snow and ice exist all year round. This varies with latitude.

Male bighorn sheep use their horns to battle over mating rights, charging at each other at speeds of 30 km/h. The horns weigh about 14 kg – more than all the other bones in its body.

GRASSLANDS

Huge grasslands are found on every continent, except Antarctica. They support enormous herds of grazing animals.

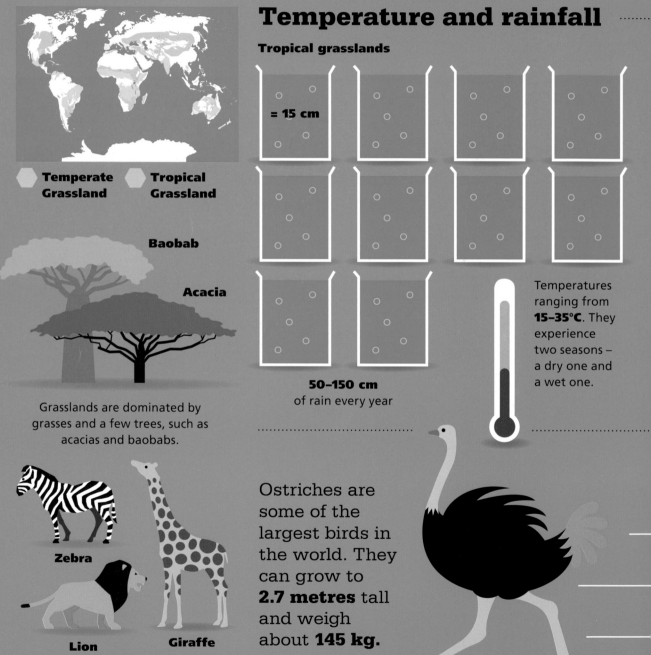

Temperate Grassland

Tropical Grassland

Baobab

Acacia

Grasslands are dominated by grasses and a few trees, such as acacias and baobabs.

Temperature and rainfall

Tropical grasslands

= 15 cm

50–150 cm of rain every year

Temperatures ranging from **15–35°C**. They experience two seasons – a dry one and a wet one.

Zebra

Lion

Giraffe

Grassland animals include buffalo, zebras, giraffes, lions, ostriches and cobras.

Ostriches are some of the largest birds in the world. They can grow to **2.7 metres** tall and weigh about **145 kg.**

The dry periods of tropical grasslands force many of the animals living there to move long distances in search of water and food. These migrations can involve millions of animals travelling hundreds of kilometres.

The Great East African migration involves more than **1.5 million wildebeest, 200,000 zebras** and **thousands of antelopes.**

Temperate grasslands

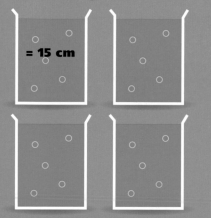

= 15 cm

30–60 cm of rain a year

Four seasons with temperatures ranging from **-10°C** in northern grasslands in January to **28°C** in July.

During every migration, about 250,000 wildebeest and 30,000 zebras are killed by predators, thirst, hunger and exhaustion.

250,000   30,000

Many plants in tropical grasslands are xerophytic. This means that they have adapted to life in dry conditions. For example, acacias have small, waxy leaves to reduce water loss.

Acacia leaves

Prairie dog

Ostriches can run at speeds of up to **70 km/h**, with each stride covering **5 metres**.

Prairie dogs are small mammals that live in the grasslands of North America. They dig burrows and live in communities called towns. Usually, these cover about 1.5 square km, but the largest ever discovered covered an area of

65,000 square km

– that's bigger than the state of West Virginia, USA. It was home to about

400,000,000

prairie dogs.

TUNDRA

Beyond the large coniferous forests and close to the polar regions is the tundra. This is a habitat where conditions are so harsh that no trees grow and where any growing season lasts a few short weeks.

⬡ **Arctic tundra**

TWO TYPES OF TUNDRA

Arctic tundra is found close to the polar regions, especially the Arctic. It covers about **10 per cent** of Earth's surface.

Alpine tundra is found high up on mountains. It covers about **3 per cent** of Earth's surface.

13%

.... Arctic Tundra

←···· Alpine Tundra

Tundra soils also act as an important store of carbon – estimates say that about **14 per cent of Earth's carbon** is tied up in the permafrost. Global warming may cause the permafrost to melt, releasing more carbon into the atmosphere.

CO_2

14%

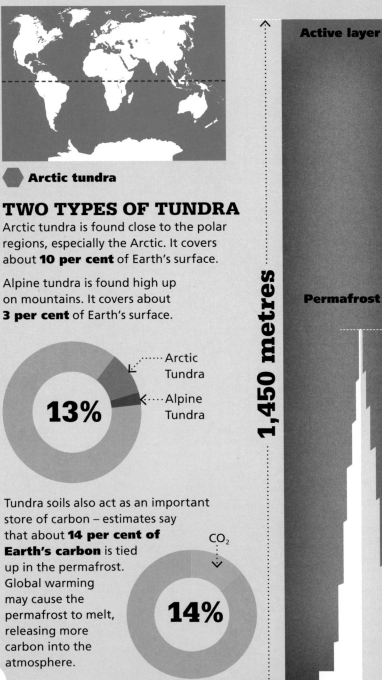

Active layer

Permafrost

1,450 metres

Burj Khalifa 830 metres

Frozen subsoil

Just beneath the Arctic tundra surface, the ground is frozen solid all year round, even in summer. This frozen layer is called permafrost. As a result, the tundra does not have animals that dig deep burrows or plants that have deep roots.

This frozen layer may stretch down **1,450 metres below the surface** in some regions – that's nearly twice the height of the Burj Khalifa in Dubai, the tallest building in the world.

Tundra is found above 60°N latitude in North America and 70°N latitude in Eurasia – the difference is caused by the warmer summers experienced on the larger landmass of Eurasia.

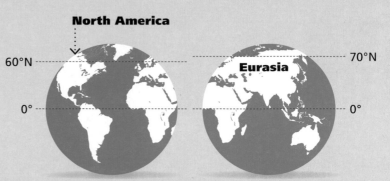

North America

60°N

0°

70°N

Eurasia

0°

Temperature and rainfall

Arctic tundra

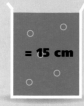

= 15 cm

Arctic tundra regions have about **38 cm** of rain a year, but can get nearly **200 cm** of snow in a year.

Temperatures range from about **4°C** in summer to **-32°C** in winter.

Alpine tundra

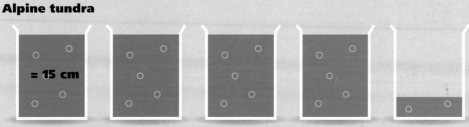

= 15 cm

Alpine tundra regions have between **7.6 cm** and **64 cm** of rain a year.

Summer temperatures can reach about **12°C** and winter temperatures descend to about **-18°C**.

The word **tundra** comes from the Finnish word **'tuntria'** which means **'treeless land'**.

Arctic poppy

Sedge

Snow goose

Wolverine

Reindeer

Tundra plants include grasses, sedges and mosses, as well as the Arctic poppy.

Tundra animals include wolverines, reindeer, musk oxen, snow geese and Arctic skuas.

THE POLES

The extreme northern and southern parts of the world are some of the most inhospitable on the planet, with freezing days and long periods of complete darkness when the Sun fails to rise above the horizon.

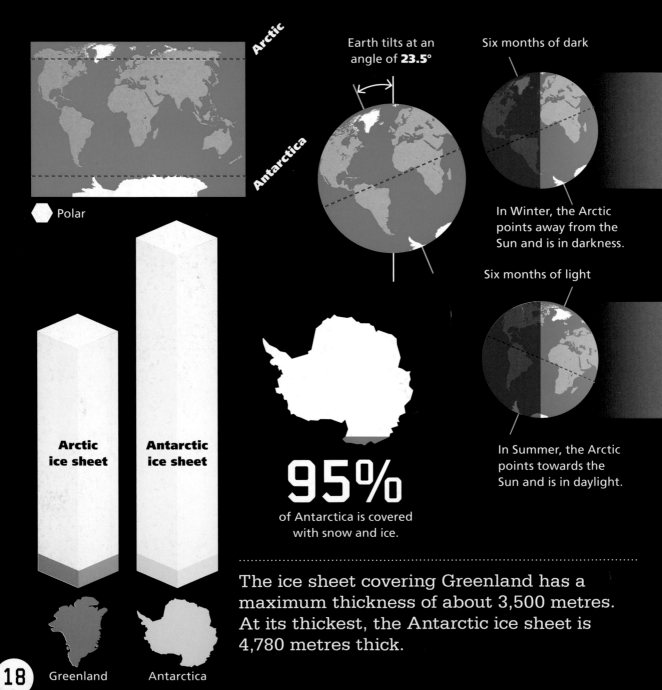

Arctic

Antarctica

Polar

Earth tilts at an angle of **23.5°**

Six months of dark

In Winter, the Arctic points away from the Sun and is in darkness.

Six months of light

In Summer, the Arctic points towards the Sun and is in daylight.

Arctic ice sheet

Antarctic ice sheet

95%

of Antarctica is covered with snow and ice.

The ice sheet covering Greenland has a maximum thickness of about 3,500 metres. At its thickest, the Antarctic ice sheet is 4,780 metres thick.

Greenland

Antarctica

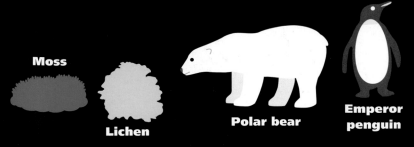

Moss

Lichen

The only plants found in these regions are small grasses, lichens and algae that can survive the harsh conditions.

Polar bear

Emperor penguin

Polar animals include polar bears, arctic foxes, crabeater seals, emperor penguins and fulmars.

Polar bears are good swimmers. One was recorded swimming for **nine days straight, covering 687 km** – that's the same distance as Washington, DC, to Boston.

Arctic sea ice levels have been decreasing. In November 2016, Arctic sea ice extent was 9.08 million sq km, the lowest November figure ever recorded – it was 1.95 million sq km lower than the average November figures for 1981–2010. That's nearly three times the size of Texas (695,621.13 sq km).

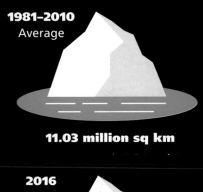

1981–2010 Average

11.03 million sq km

2016

9.08 million sq km

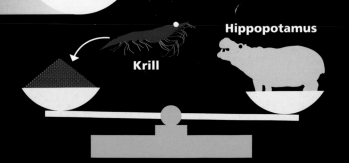

Hippopotamus

Krill

Every year, huge amounts of tiny plankton flourish in Antarctic waters, attracting some of the biggest creatures on the planet. In a single day, an adult blue whale will eat about 40 million tiny krill, weighing in at more than **3,500 kg of food** – that's about the same weight as a hippopotamus!

The lowest ever temperature was recorded at Vostok Station in Antarctica. It was

-89.2°C.

Since 1960, average winter temperatures on the Antarctic Peninsula have increased by 10.8°C.

COASTS

Coasts are where the sea meets the land. This creates a habitat that changes regularly as the seas rise and fall with the tides and where features are carved out by the power of the ocean.

The world has about

620,000 KM
of coastline

– almost long enough to stretch **to the Moon and back**.

Nearly 2.4 billion people, about one-third of the world's population, live within 100 km of the coast.

15 M

– the greatest tidal range, found at the Bay of Fundy, Canada, equivalent to a three-storey house.

Current sea level

Sea level last ice age period

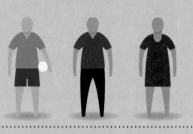

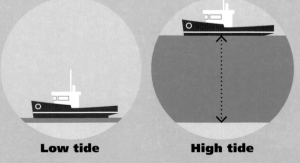

Low tide   **High tide**

TIDES
The daily rise and fall of sea levels is caused by the gravitational pull of the Moon and Sun on the water.

During the last ice age period, sea levels were more than 120 metres lower than today – almost the height of **the Great Pyramid at Giza** (originally 130 metres).

Waves can hit with
a pressure of

500 KG

per sq cm.

This force can create a
wide range of diverse
features. These include:

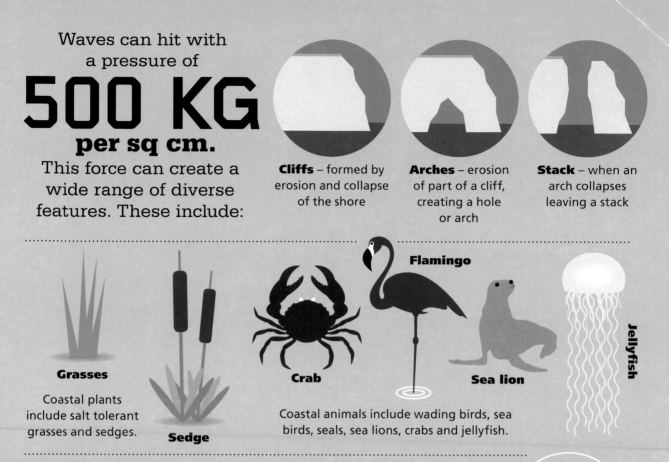

Cliffs – formed by
erosion and collapse
of the shore

Arches – erosion
of part of a cliff,
creating a hole
or arch

Stack – when an
arch collapses
leaving a stack

Flamingo

Jellyfish

Grasses

Coastal plants
include salt tolerant
grasses and sedges.

Sedge

Crab

Sea lion

Coastal animals include wading birds, sea
birds, seals, sea lions, crabs and jellyfish.

Coral reefs

Coral reefs are formed from the
rocky skeletons of tiny creatures,
called polyps. Some of the reefs
today started forming about
50 million years ago.

Coral Polyp

Polyps are translucent (see-through)
– they get their colours from brightly
coloured algae called zooxanthellae.

Great Barrier Reef

The world's largest coral reef is the
Great Barrier Reef off the coast
of Australia. It stretches for more
than 2,600 km and covers an area
about half the size of Texas, USA.

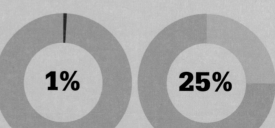

1%

25%

Coral reefs cover less than 1 per cent
of the ocean floor, but they support about
25 per cent of all marine creatures.

WETLANDS

Wetlands are regions where the ground is waterlogged for at least part of the year. These habitats are found close to the sea, where saltwater floods the ground, or further inland in freshwater bogs, marshes and swamps.

Types of wetland

Mangroves

These wetlands are named after the trees that grow in them. They have long stilt roots that stand out of the mud and keep the plant above the water. They also have special respiratory roots, called pneumatophores, which stick above the mud and water and have small openings to let air in.

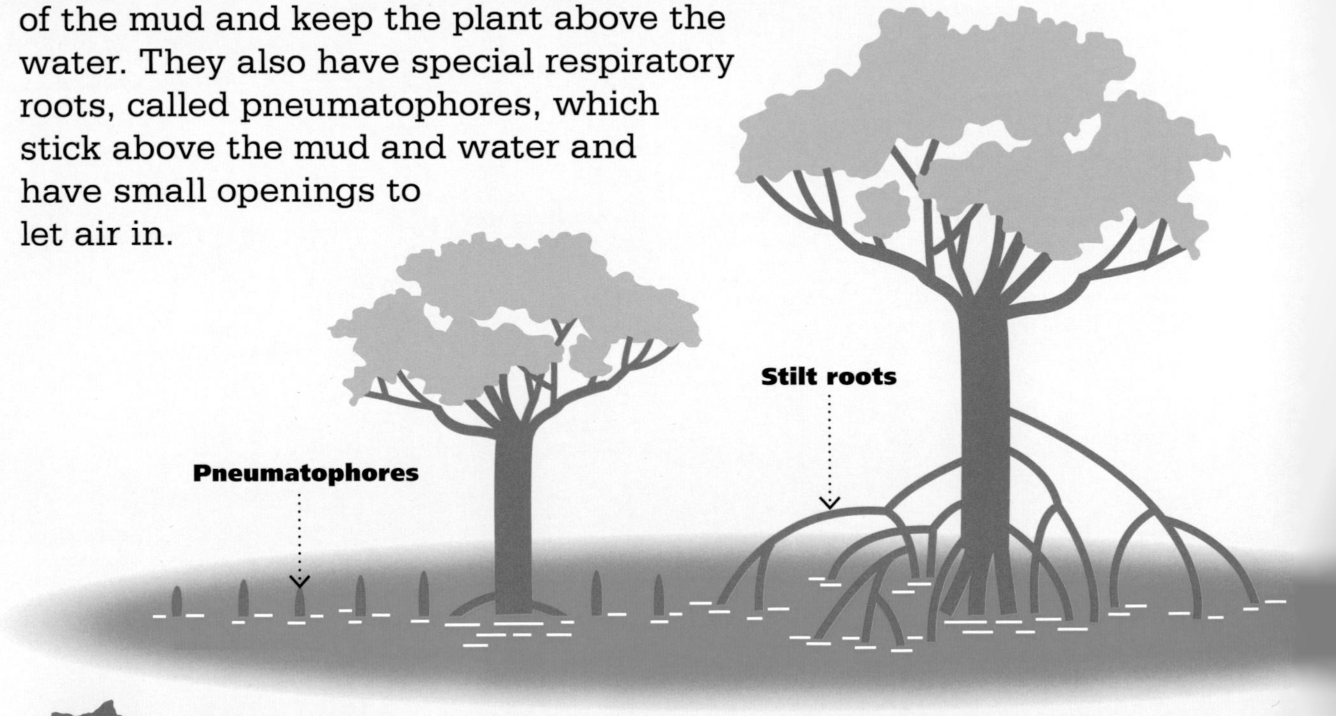

Stilt roots

Pneumatophores

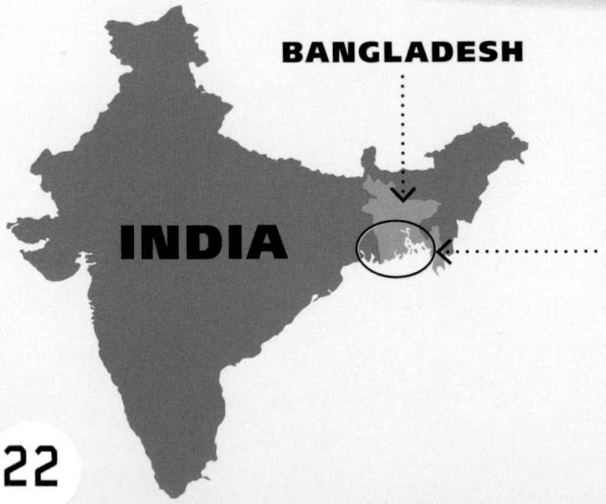

BANGLADESH

INDIA

The Sundarbans in India and Bangladesh is one of the largest saltwater swamps on the planet, covering about

10,000 SQ KM
– THAT'S ABOUT THE SAME SIZE AS THE ISLAND OF HAWAII.

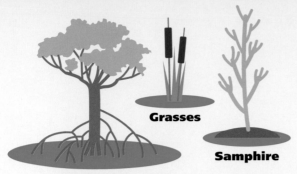

Mangroves

Grasses

Samphire

Wetland plants include mangroves, grasses and samphire.

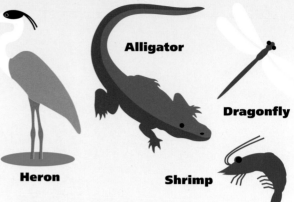

Alligator

Dragonfly

Heron

Shrimp

Wetland animals include catfish, wading birds, shrimp, dragonflies and alligators.

Tidal marshes

These are found on river systems that are close enough to the coast to have their waters rise and fall every day with the ocean tides.

Freshwater marshes

These form in areas where water collects and cannot drain away easily. They range in size from small potholes to huge regions, such as the Florida Everglades, USA, which covers about 1,900 sq km.

Riparian wetlands

These are formed when a river overflows and floods the surrounding area. Every year, the waters of the Amazon flood up to 250,000 square km, an area the size of the state of Michigan, USA.

Peatlands

Peatlands form when material from dead plants and animals decomposes slowly and starts to build up. This forms a layer of peat, which contains a high level of organic matter.

RIVERS AND LAKES

Rain falling on high ground and spring water that bubbles up from underground flow downhill and collect into channels to form streams. These join together to create rivers, which flow into lakes or the sea.

Profile of a river

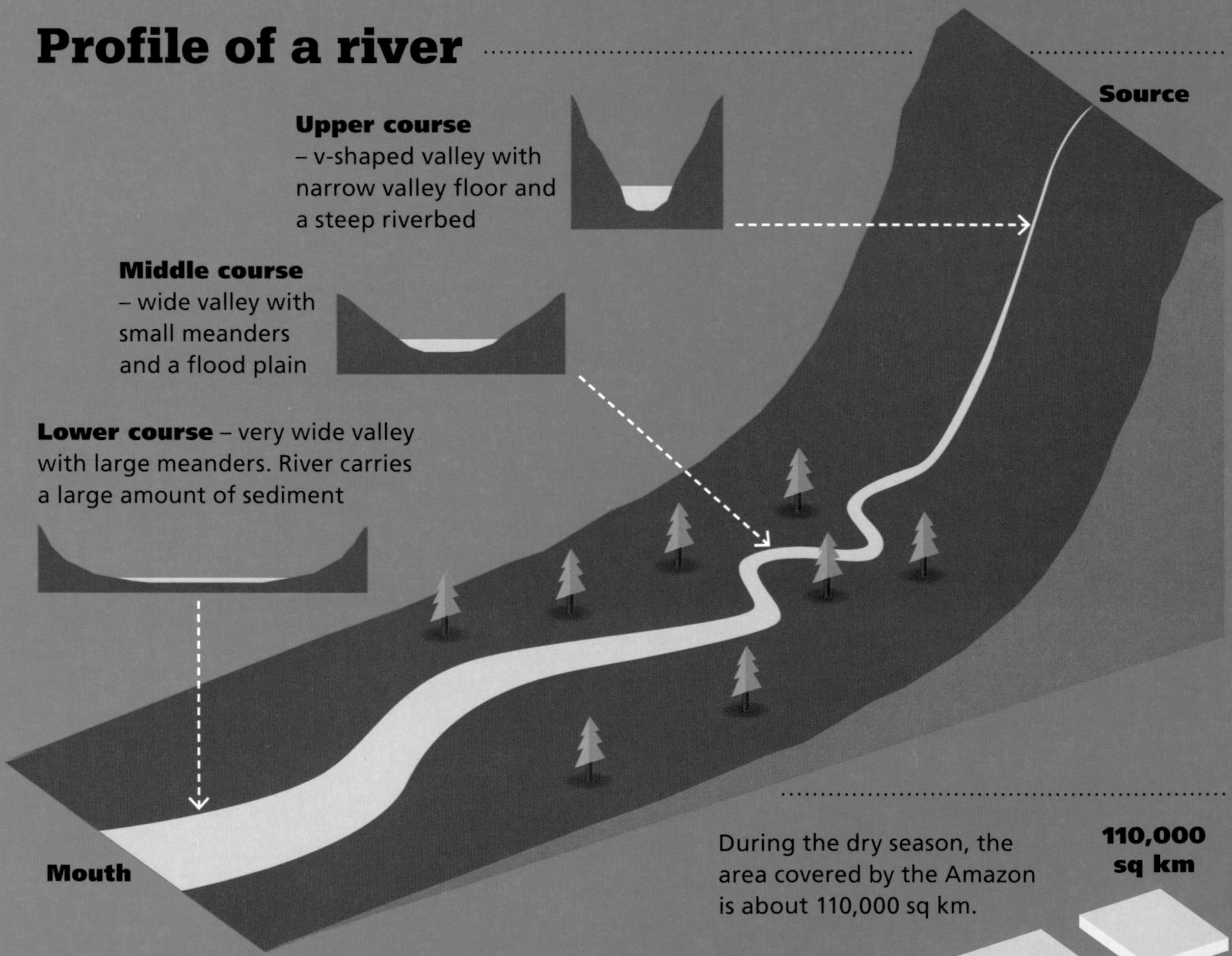

Source

Upper course – v-shaped valley with narrow valley floor and a steep riverbed

Middle course – wide valley with small meanders and a flood plain

Lower course – very wide valley with large meanders. River carries a large amount of sediment

Mouth

During the dry season, the area covered by the Amazon is about 110,000 sq km.

110,000 sq km

350,000 sq km

In the wet season, this increases to about 350,000 sq km.

The Amazon is the widest river in the world. At times it can be 40 km across, which is wider than the English Channel.

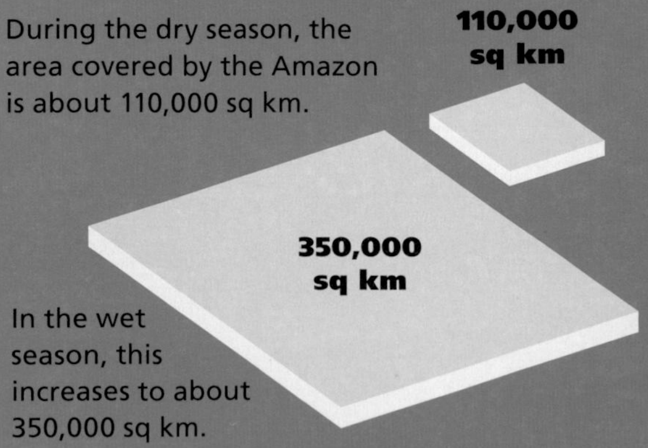

RUSSIA

Lake Baikal

Lake Baikal in Russia is the largest lake in the world.

Its maximum depth is

1,620 M.

DEEP ENOUGH TO SWALLOW THE EMPIRE STATE BUILDING **MORE THAN 3.5 TIMES.**

It holds 23,000 cubic km of water **– about one-fifth of the world's freshwater.**

<...... **World's freshwater**

<...... **Lake Baikal**

There are about

117 MILLION
LAKES ON EARTH

and about **90 million of these (about 77 per cent)** cover less than 1 hectare – less area than two American football fields.

When combined, the shorelines of the world's lakes measure **250 times** the distance around the Equator.

Duck

Crocodile

River dolphin

Freshwater animals include otters, river dolphins, water birds, such as ducks and geese, freshwater fish, such as sturgeon, crocodiles and frogs.

Sturgeon are the largest freshwater fish in the world. The biggest ever recorded was **6 metres long and weighed more than 3,000 kg.**

Water lilies

Freshwater plants include water lilies.

OCEANS

Seas and oceans cover more than 70 per cent of our planet. They offer a broad range of habitats, from the deep ocean to shallow seas.

Pressure

Surface

1,000 m

CRUSHING PRESSURES

The average depth of the ocean is 3,800 metres. The deepest part of the ocean is Challenger Deep, which is 10,994 metres below sea level. Pressures here are 1,000 times greater than at sea level.

Average depth
3,800 m

x500

5,000 m

x1,000

10,000 m

Challenger Deep
10,994 m

SWIRLING CURRENTS

Huge ocean currents carry cold and warm water around the globe, spreading heat and maintaining different habitats on land and sea.

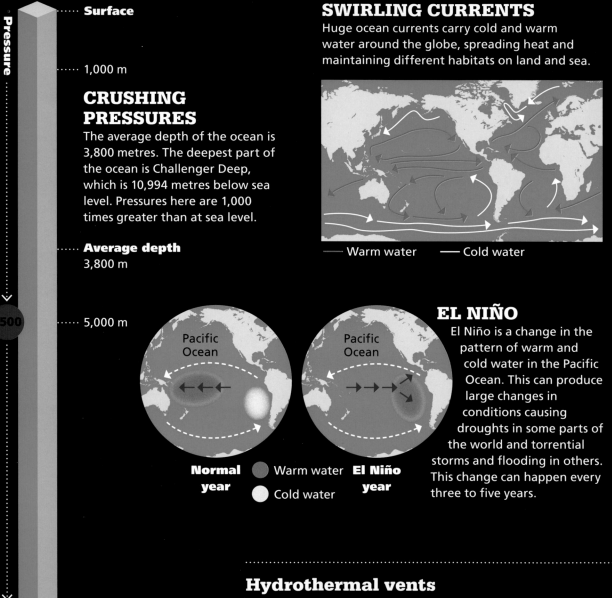

—— Warm water   —— Cold water

Pacific Ocean

Pacific Ocean

EL NIÑO

El Niño is a change in the pattern of warm and cold water in the Pacific Ocean. This can produce large changes in conditions causing droughts in some parts of the world and torrential storms and flooding in others. This change can happen every three to five years.

Normal year   ● Warm water   **El Niño year**
             ● Cold water

Hydrothermal vents

These are areas where super-hot water gushes out from the seafloor. The hot water is rich in nutrients and minerals and attracts some unique wildlife.

Ocean giants
Seas and oceans are home to some of the biggest animals on the planet:

Lion's mane jellyfish – about 35 metres long

Blue whale – about 30 metres long

Giant squid – about 12 metres long

Whale shark – about 13 metres long

Oarfish – about 8 metres long

Ocean sunfish – about 2.5 metres long

Japanese spider crab – about 3.7 metres across

Giant clam – about 1.4 metres across

400°C
– the temperature of water gushing out of a hydrothermal vent.

Giant tube worms live on hydrothermal vents and can be 2–3 metres long.

Giant kelp – up to 30 metres

Giraffe – up to 6 metres

Towering plants
Giant kelp is a giant seaweed, which is a type of algae. It attaches to the sea floor in cool, clear waters and stretches up for 30 metres. It grows in thick forests that are home to thousands of animal species, such as sea otters.

ARTIFICIAL HABITATS

They may look like harsh habitats where few wild plants and animals could survive, but many living things have adapted to thrive in urban environments, living close to thousands of people. And towns and cities are one of the few habitats that are increasing in size.

Growing habitat

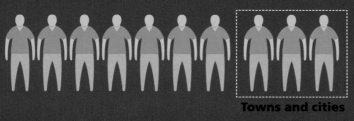

Towns and cities

In 1950, about one-third of the world's population lived in towns and cities.

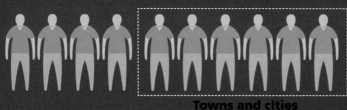

Towns and cities

By 2030, a projected two-thirds of the world's population with be living in towns and cities.

IN 1950, THERE WERE JUST TWO MEGACITIES, WITH POPULATIONS OF MORE THAN 10 MILLION.

TODAY, THERE ARE 21 MEGACITIES.

RICH HABITATS

Even a small back garden will have a rich variety of wildlife. A study of a garden in Sheffield, UK, found:

More than 1,000 plant species

80 species of lichen

4,000 species of invertebrates

WILDLIFE CORRIDORS

To promote wildlife conservation, corridors of grasslands and woodlands can be built from one wildlife habitat to another so that animals can move freely.

285

– the number of bird species that have been spotted in New York's Central Park.

PERFECT PERCH

Skyscrapers offer an ideal spot for falcons and other birds of prey to nest. They also give the birds a good view of the surrounding area in their hunt for food.

There are an estimated

4,000,000

rats living in Paris

– almost twice the human population (2.2 million).

ARTIFICIAL REEFS

These are man-made structures that are deliberately sunk so that marine plants and animals can grow on them. One of the biggest was the aircraft carrier USS *Oriskany* which was more than 270 metres long. It was sunk on 17 May 2006.

GLOSSARY

algae
Simple plants that usually live in water. They include seaweeds.

altitude
The height of something in relation to sea level or ground level.

baobab
A short tree with a very thick trunk and large edible fruit, common in grassland regions.

canopy
The highest branches of trees in a forest.

carbon
A chemical found in coal, for example, that can be harmful to the atmosphere. Trees and permafrost absorb carbon.

climate
The weather of an area over a long period.

coniferous
Something that is made up of or related to conifer trees, such as a coniferous forest.

deciduous
A type of plant, such as a tree, shrub or bush, that loses its leaves in autumn every year.

desertification
The process in which fertile land becomes desert as a result of drought, deforestation or poor farming methods.

drought
A long period without rain, leading to water shortages and crop failures.

evergreen
A type of plant that keeps its leaves all year.

grasslands
Large open regions covered in grass and often used for grazing.

habitat
The natural home of an animal or plant.

hibernation
When an animal or plant spends the winter in a dormant or sleep-like state.

ice age
A long period of low temperatures on the Earth's surface, causing the expansion of polar ice sheets and glaciers.

liana
A long, woody vine that grows from the ground and climbs up trees to reach the forest canopy.

megacity
A very large city with a population of more than 10 million. Mumbai in India and Shanghai in China are examples of megacities.

migration
The movement of animals between places.

permafrost
A layer of soil beneath the surface of the ground, which remains frozen all year.

plankton
Microscopic organisms that drift in water.

pnuematophores
Specialised roots that poke above water and help plants to breathe in waterlogged soil.

precipitation
Rain, snow, sleet or hail that fall to the ground.

respiration
The process that uses oxygen and sugars to produce energy, water and carbon dioxide.

samphire
A plant similar to parsley that grows on rocks and cliffs near the sea.

sea ice
Frozen seawater that floats on the water's surface. Sea ice covers about 12 per cent of the world's oceans.

sedge
A grass-like plant that grows in wet ground in temperate and cold regions.

stilt roots
Supporting roots that prevent shallow-rooted trees from falling over and hold the plant above any floodwater.

taiga
The swampy regions of coniferous forest found in northern latitudes.

temperate
Refers to the parts of the world that lie between the tropics and the poles.

tidal range
The measurement difference between high tide and low tide.

tropical
Refers to parts of the world that lie on either side of the Equator.

tundra
A vast, flat, treeless Arctic region of Europe, Asia and North America in which the subsoil is permanently frozen.

xerophyte
A plant that has adapted to live in an area with very little water, such as a desert.

Websites

MORE INFO:
primaryhomeworkhelp.co.uk/habitats.html
A web page packed full of amazing facts and information about habitats and how plants and animals are adapted to live in them.

interactivesites.weebly.com/habitats.html
This website provides links to other websites with activities and information on habitats.

australianmuseum.net.au/wild-kids-habitats
A website with information and explanations of different types of habitat from around the world.

MORE GRAPHICS:
www.visualinformation.info
A website that contains a whole host of infographic material on subjects as diverse as natural history, science, sport and computer games.

www.coolinfographics.com
A collection of infographics and data visualisations from other online resources, magazines and newspapers.

www.dailyinfographic.com
A comprehensive collection of infographics on an enormous range of topics that is updated every single day!

INDEX

ACKNOWLEDGEMENTS

First published in Great Britain
in 2017 by Wayland
Copyright © Wayland, 2017
All rights reserved

Editor: Hayley Shortt
Produced by Tall Tree Ltd
Editor: Jon Richards
Designer: Ed Simkins

ISBN: 978 1 5263 0355 4
10 9 8 7 6 5 4 3 2 1

Wayland
An imprint of Hachette
Children's Group
Part of Hodder and Stoughton
Carmelite House
50 Victoria Embankment
London EC4Y 0DZ

An Hachette UK Company
www.hachette.co.uk
www.hachettechildrens.co.uk

Printed and bound in China

The website addresses (URLs) included in this
book were valid at the time of going to press.
However, it is possible that contents or
addresses may have changed since the
publication of this book. No responsibility
for any such changes can be accepted by
either the author or the Publisher.

MIX
Paper from
responsible sources
FSC® C104740

GET THE PICTURE!

Welcome to the world of **infographics!** Icons, pictograms and graphics create an exciting form of data visualisation, presenting information in a new and appealing way.

9780750278461 — the world in infographics — PLANET EARTH

9780750278454 — SPACE

9780750283069 — the world in infographics — COUNTRIES

9780750281287 — the world in infographics — MACHINES AND VEHICLES

9780750278683 — the world in infographics — THE HUMAN BODY

9780750283205 — NATURAL RESOURCES

9780750269049 — the world in infographics — THE HUMAN WORLD

9780750283199 — the world in infographics — ANIMAL KINGDOM

9780750277792 — the world in infographics — SPORT

9780750269032 — the world in infographics — THE NATURAL WORLD

9780750279628 — ART AND ENTERTAINMENT

9780750283076 — TECHNOLOGY

9780750298407 — history in infographics — ANCIENT EGYPTIANS

9781526398391 — history in infographics — THE MAYANS

9781526300225 — THE STONE AGE

9781526300249 — history in infographics — THE VIKINGS